NOV   2014

You Want Me to Eat That?

▪ A KIDS' GUIDE TO EATING RIGHT ▪

by Rachelle Kreisman

with illustrations by Tim Haggerty

RED
CHAIR
▪PRESS▪

Please visit our website at **www.redchairpress.com** for more high-quality products for young readers.

For a free activity page for this story, go to
www.redchairpress.com and look for Free Activities.

You Want Me To Eat That?

Publisher's Cataloging-In-Publication Data
(Prepared by The Donohue Group, Inc.)

Kreisman, Rachelle, author.

You want me to eat that? : a kids' guide to eating right / by Rachelle Kreisman ; with illustrations by Tim Haggerty.

pages : illustrations ; cm. -- (Start smart: health)

Includes bibliographical references and index.

Summary: Have you ever heard, "Eat your vegetables?" Some of the orange ones are okay; even the yellow ones are fine. Give it a chance and discover why a variety of foods is good for building strong bodies and brains.
ISBN: 978-1-937529-71-0 (library hardcover)
ISBN: 978-1-937529-70-3 (paperback)
ISBN: 978-1-937529-90-1 (ebook)

1. Children--Nutrition--Juvenile literature. 2. Nutrition. I. Haggerty, Tim, illustrator. II. Title.

RA784 .K74 2014

613.2/083   2013956245

Illustration credits: p. 1, 5, 7, 9, 10, 11, 13, 14, 15, 16, 19, 20, 23, 25, 27, 29, 30: Tim Haggerty; p. 8: Scott MacNeill

Photo credits: Cover: © Rubber Ball Productions/Getty Images; p. 6, 7, 10, 11, 12, 17, 20, 25: IStock; p. 23: Dreamstime; p. 5, 8, 9, 11, 14, 18, 21, 22, 23, 24, 26: Shutterstock; p.32: Courtesy of the author, Rachel Kreisman

This series first published by:
Red Chair Press LLC   PO Box 333   South Egremont, MA 01258-0333

Printed in the United States of America

1 2 3 4 5 18 17 16 15 14

Table of Contents

Words in **bold type** are defined in the glossary.

CHAPTER 1

Fuel Up

*R**umble. Rumble. Growl.** Do you hear that? It's not an earthquake or a tiger. That sound is your stomach saying, "Feed me!" Why so hungry? Your body needs food to work properly. Not just any kind of food will do. Your body craves healthful foods. They contain **nutrients**. Nutrients are the good things found in food that people need to live.

It's not me! That's your stomach growling!

Your body works hard. It needs lots of nutrients to keep it going. They help your body grow, heal, and fight germs. Nutrients also give you brain power.

And that's not all! Nutrients give you energy to move too. Thanks to nutrients in food, you can run, play, do chores— and live a healthful life.

JUST JOKING!

Q: Why shouldn't you tell a secret on a farm?

A: Because the corn has ears and the potatoes have eyes.

Choosing the right foods to eat is important. Some foods have more nutrients than others. Candy bars, chips, and cookies don't have many nutrients. Instead they are often full of sugar and fat. Too much fat and sugar are bad for you. That's why these types of foods are sometimes called junk food.

Give up junk foods and choose healthful foods that taste good and have lots of nutrients. Fruits and vegetables such as apples and carrots are two good examples. But there are many more tasty foods to choose from every day.

A healthy diet is balanced. It is made up of a variety of foods. Each food supplies your body with different nutrients. For example, milk and cheese make your bones stronger. Meat helps you build muscle. Oranges can help your body heal cuts.

Water is a big part of a healthy diet, too. Drink plenty of it during the day. Drink extra water on hot days and when you are being active.

FUN FACT!

Water makes up more than half of your body weight!

CHAPTER 2

Food Groups

What is the magic number for a healthy diet? Five! A healthy diet is made up of foods from five groups. They are fruits, vegetables, grains, protein, and dairy.

You can see the five food groups on the food plate below. It shows how much to eat from each food group.

Dairy

Fruits

Grains

Vegetables

Protein

♥ MyPlate shows you how to have a balanced diet.

Sweet! Fruits are known as nature's candy. They are very good for you. Fruits are full of **vitamins** and **minerals**. Those nutrients help keep your eyes, skin, teeth, gums, and heart healthy. Kids need between 1 and 1 ½ cups of fruit each day.

Eat a variety of fresh, dried, or frozen fruits each day. Snack on apples, bananas, mangoes, and berries. You can even drink your fruit as juice.

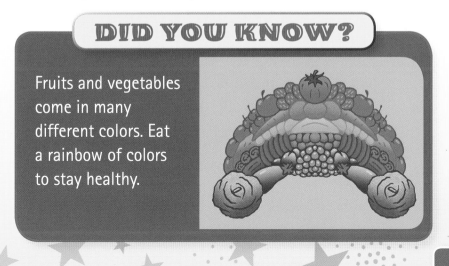

DID YOU KNOW?

Fruits and vegetables come in many different colors. Eat a rainbow of colors to stay healthy.

Grab some vegetables and enjoy! With so many choices, it's hard to decide what to eat first. Munch on broccoli, celery, and red peppers. Make a salad with lettuce and tomatoes. Then toss in some chickpeas. Enjoy sweet potatoes, beets, and corn.

Vegetables are loaded with vitamins and minerals. Most kids need between 1 ½ and 2 ½ cups of veggies each day. Eat them raw or cooked. Yum!

FUN FACT!

More than 60 vegetables are commonly eaten. How many different kinds of vegetables have you tried? Make a list and count them. Have you tried more than 20 types?

The grains group gives you energy. Grains are foods made from plant seeds. Some grains are oats, rice, wheat, cornmeal, and barley. The best grains for you are whole grains. They contain the whole seed. These grains are rich in **fiber**. Fiber helps your body digest food and keeps your insides healthy.

Kids need 5 to 6 ounces of grains each day. Make sure half of those grains are whole grains. Try whole-wheat bread, oatmeal, and plain popcorn.

DID YOU KNOW?

Fruits and veggies are also good sources of fiber.

FIBER

Protein keeps your body strong. It builds and repairs your muscles, bones, skin, blood, and **organs**. Protein comes from animals and plants. Seafood, meat, and eggs are animal sources. Beans, peas, nuts, and seeds are plant sources. Kids need 4 to 5 ounces of protein a day.

Which protein food rhymes with wish? Fish! Eat fish at least twice a week. Try salmon, sardines, and trout. They are extra good for your heart.

♥ Salmon are found in freshwater and in the cold northern ocean waters. Salmon is a tasty meal!

In a *moo*-vie about dairy, cows would be the stars. That is because milk and foods made from milk are dairy foods. They contain the mineral **calcium**. Calcium is a nutrient. It builds strong bones and teeth.

Foods made from milk can be high in fat. Eating too much fat is not healthy. Have low-fat milk, low-fat yogurt, and low-fat cheese. Kids need 2 ½ to 3 cups of dairy foods each day.

DID YOU KNOW?

Some kids are allergic to dairy. The good news is that calcium is found in other foods. Almond milk and broccoli are rich in calcium. Cereals and orange juice can also have added calcium.

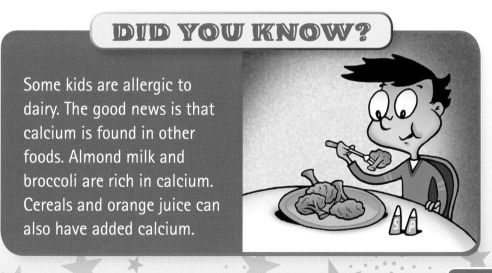

Fat is not a food group. But your body still needs some of it. Oil is a liquid fat that comes from fish and plants. Oil contains nutrients that your body needs. It also helps your body **absorb** certain vitamins.

Go nuts! Walnuts, almonds and other nuts contain good oils. But many people are allergic to nuts. So another way to get healthful oils is to eat fish, avocadoes, and olives. Olive oil and lemon are good to use on a salad and both are good for you. A little oil each day is all your body needs.

You have so many healthful food choices! Each food group gives your body nutrients. They all contain vitamins and minerals too. What can a few vitamins and minerals do? (Hint: You already know about calcium.) Check out the chart below to learn more.

Vitamin or Mineral	How It Helps	Found In
Vitamin A	helps your vision	carrots, sweet potatoes, spinach
Vitamin C	helps wounds heal	oranges, broccoli, strawberries
Vitamin D	helps your body absorb calcium	salmon, sardines, milk, eggs
Vitamin K	stops cuts from bleeding	spinach, broccoli, kale, cabbage
Calcium	builds strong bones and teeth	milk, cheese, yogurt, broccoli
Iron	helps your blood carry oxygen	beans, beef, spinach, some cereals

FUN FACT!

Your body can make its own vitamin D. Sunlight on your skin does the trick. About 10 minutes of sun a few times a week is often enough to give your body all the vitamin D it needs. If you are going to be outside longer, put on sunscreen to protect your skin.

CHAPTER 3

Use It or Lose It

What happens to food once you put it in your mouth? Here is a look at what takes place from start to finish.

You take a bite with your teeth and chew the food. As you chew, your mouth makes more **saliva** so the food gets mushy which helps you to swallow it. Your tongue pushes the mushy food down your throat and into your **esophagus** (eh-SAH-fuh-guhs). It is about 10-inches long and shaped like a tube.

Muscles in your esophagus squeeze the food down. The next stop is the stomach. There, food gets mixed and mashed. Juices in your stomach turn the food into a liquid.

The liquid food travels to the small **intestine**. It is a long tube that curls around and around. If it were straight, it would be about 20 feet long! That's longer than a car!

Your Digestive System

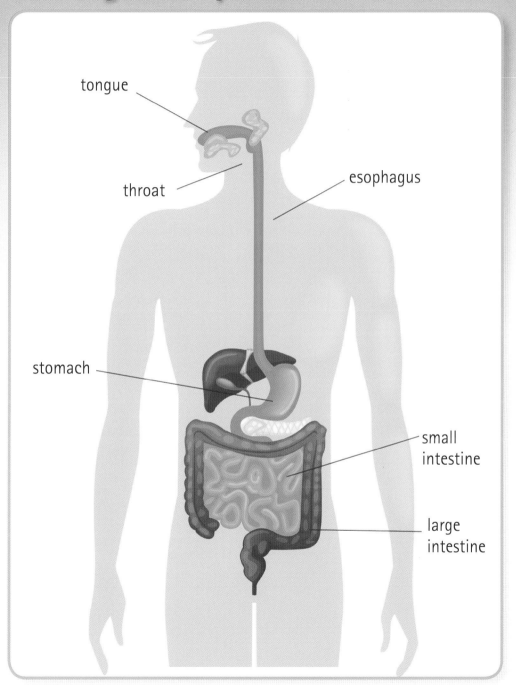

tongue

throat

esophagus

stomach

small intestine

large intestine

Juices in your small intestine break down the food some more. It gets separated into nutrients. Special **cells** collect the nutrients. Tiny blood vessels in the small intestine pick them up. Blood carries the nutrients around your body. Do your bones need more calcium?

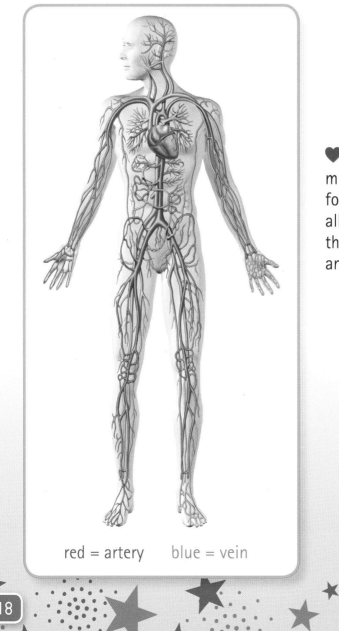

red = artery   blue = vein

♥ Vitamins and minerals from the food you eat reach all parts of your body through your veins and arteries

Help is on the way! Do you have a cut on your finger? Vitamin K to the rescue! It helps stop the cut from bleeding.

Your body can't use some parts of the food you eat. The waste travels to your large intestine. Don't be fooled by the name. The large intestine is only about five feet long. It gets its name because it is wider than the much longer small intestine.

In the large intestine, waste becomes more solid. It then moves to the **rectum**. There, the waste gets ready to leave your body as poop. And that is where the food journey ends.

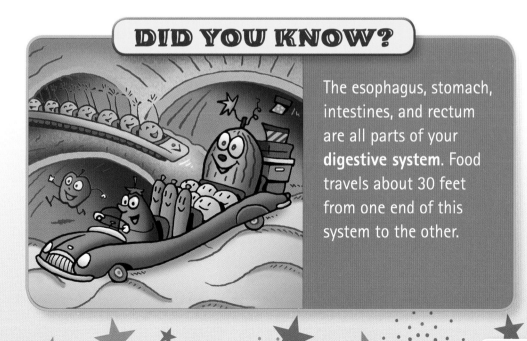

DID YOU KNOW?

The esophagus, stomach, intestines, and rectum are all parts of your **digestive system**. Food travels about 30 feet from one end of this system to the other.

Good-Health Tips

Good morning! Are you hungry? That is no surprise. Your stomach is empty after a long night's sleep. What is the best way to start the day? Eat a healthy breakfast! It is the most important meal of the day because it helps your body get ready for all that you will be doing. Breakfast gives you energy and the fuel you need to do well in school.

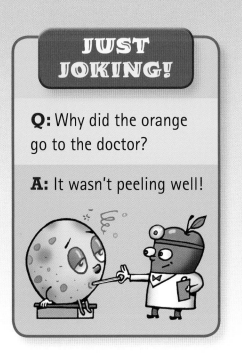

JUST JOKING!

Q: Why did the orange go to the doctor?

A: It wasn't peeling well!

♥ Breakfast gives you fuel to start your day.

What can't you eat for breakfast? Lunch and dinner! Your body needs food throughout the day. If you are hungry between meals, have a healthy snack instead of junk food.

Munch on plain popcorn instead of potato chips. Trade those cookies for a granola bar. Do you feel like a cold treat? Say "hello" to a frozen fruit smoothie instead of ice cream.

Eating at a restaurant can be fun. It can also be tricky. How do you know what to order? Stay away from fried foods, such as fried chicken and French fries. They are full of unhealthy fats. Choose grilled, steamed, and baked foods instead.

Is soda pop on the menu? If so, say "No, thanks!" Soda pop and other sugary drinks are not good for you. They don't contain many nutrients. Drink water, fruit juice, or low-fat milk instead.

At the end of the meal, the chocolate cake is calling your name. Dessert is fine to have once in a while. You can also eat less by sharing it with someone else. That is a win-win for both of you. Try yogurt and berries to get dairy and good-for-you fruit!

DID YOU KNOW?

Too much sugar can damage teeth. If you eat a sugary treat, make sure to brush your teeth after.

Here are some more good-health tips about food and eating. Chew slowly and enjoy your food. Then stop eating when you feel full.

You will feel your best if you eat on a regular schedule. If you wait too long between meals, you may get so hungry that you will eat more than you need. That can make you gain too much weight. Being very overweight can lead to health problems.

Potatoes may be good for you. Being a couch potato is not. So, get up and move! Kids need at least 60 minutes of exercise each day.

Being active builds strong bones and muscles and helps you look and feel good. Exercise burns fat, which helps keep your body at a healthy weight.

Heart-pumping exercise, such as running, jumping rope, biking, or playing sports makes your heart strong. That helps it pump blood and carry nutrients to every part of your body.

TRY THIS!

Walk for five minutes while singing a song. Now run or jog for several minutes and try to sing. That is not easy to do. Why? Heart-pumping exercises, such as running, make you breathe faster and harder. Your lungs are taking in more **oxygen**.

Well, look at that! You have a healthy meal on your plate. Give yourself a high five. That's right—a high five! Why? You remembered the five food groups. Your body will be full of nutrients and energy soon. You can use that energy to get active! Don't keep your stomach waiting. Go ahead and enjoy your meal!

What You Can Do!

How many of these rules do you follow? Count the number of things you do. See how you score below.

You . . .

1. eat meals on a regular schedule.
2. fill your plate with fruits and veggies.
3. drink water throughout the day.
4. stop eating when you feel full.
5. eat plenty of whole grains.
6. eat foods that contain calcium.
7. start the day with breakfast.
8. eat a variety of healthy foods.
9. have a well-balanced diet.
10. exercise for 60 minutes a day.

If you answered "yes" to . . .

* **eight or more** — Great job eating healthy!

* **five to seven** — You are almost there.

* **one to four** — Keep trying. You can do it!

Glossary

absorb: to take in

calcium: a mineral that builds strong bones and teeth

cells: tiny building blocks of each living thing

digestive system: the body's system that digests, or uses, food

esophagus: the tube that carries food from the throat to the stomach

fiber: the parts of food from plants that pass through the body

intestine: the tube (made up of the small and large intestine) where food travels after leaving the stomach

minerals: nutrients that people need to stay healthy

nutrients: the good things found in food that people need to grow and live

organ: a body part, such as the heart or stomach, that has a certain job to do

oxygen: a gas in the air that people need to live

rectum: the end of the large intestine

saliva: a liquid made in the mouth that keeps it wet

vitamins: nutrients that people need to stay healthy

What Did You Learn?

See how much you learned about eating healthy.
Answer *true* or *false* for each statement below.
Write your answers on a separate piece of paper.

1. Eating a balanced diet is good for your health.
   True or false?

2. The oils group is one of the five food groups.
   True or false?

3. Most kids don't need to eat protein each day.
   True or false?

4. Some sugars build strong bones and teeth.
   True or false?

5. Blood carries nutrients around your body.
   True or false?

Answers: 1. True, 2. False (The five food groups are fruits, vegetables, grains, protein, and dairy.), 3. False (Kids need to eat 4 or 5 ounces of protein each day.), 4. False (Calcium, not sugar, builds strong bones and teeth), 5. True

For More Information

Books

Doeden, Matt. *Eat Right!* (Health Zone) Lerner, 2009.

Levete, Sarah. *Let's Talk About Eating and Health.* Aladdin Books Ltd, 2006.

Miller, Edward. *The Monster Health Book: A Guide to Eating Healthy, Being Active & Feeling Great for Monsters & Kids.* Holiday House, 2006.

Petrie, Kristin. *The Digestive System.* Abdo Consulting Group, Inc., 2007.

Rockwell, Lizzy. *Good Enough to Eat: A Kid's Guide to Food and Nutrition.* HarperCollins Publishers, 1999.

Sears, William. *Eat Healthy, Feel Great.* Little, Brown and Company, 2002.

Web Sites

BAM! Body and Mind:
http://www.cdc.gov/bam/nutrition

GirlsHealth.gov:
http://www.girlshealth.gov/nutrition

KidsHealth:
http://kidshealth.org/kid/stay_healthy

SuperKids Nutrition:
http://www.superkidsnutrition.com

USDA: MyPlate Kids' Place:
http://www.choosemyplate.gov/kids

Note to educators and parents: Our editors have carefully reviewed these web sites to ensure they are suitable for children. Web sites change frequently, however, and we cannot guarantee that a site's future contents will continue to meet our high standards of quality and educational value. You may wish to preview these sites and closely supervise children whenever they access the Internet.

Index

About the Author

Rachelle Kreisman has been a children's writer and editor for many years. She wrote hundreds of classroom magazines for *Weekly Reader*. Those issues included health topics about nutrition, illness prevention, sports safety, and fitness. When Rachelle is not writing, she enjoys being active. She likes taking walks, hiking, biking, kayaking, and doing yoga.